# The Micro World of
# ATOMS AND MOLECULES

by Precious McKenzie

CAPSTONE PRESS
a capstone imprint

Published by Capstone Press, an imprint of Capstone
1710 Roe Crest Drive, North Mankato, Minnesota 56003
capstonepub.com

Library of Congress Cataloging-in-Publication Data is available on the Library of Congress website
ISBN: 9781663976857 (hardcover)
ISBN: 9781666320992 (paperback)
ISBN: 9781666321005 (ebook PDF)

Summary: All the things people can see and touch in the universe are made up of atoms. Atoms contain electrons, protons, and neutrons. They are so tiny they cannot be seen without special microscopes. Discover the parts of atoms, how atoms join to form molecules, and their role in the periodic table of elements.

Editorial Credits
Editor: Arnold Ringstad; Designer: Sarah Taplin; Production Specialists: Joshua Olson and Laura Manthe


Content Consultant
Christina Bagwill, PhD, Assistant Professor, Chemistry Department, Saint Louis University


Image Credits
Getty Images: anilyanik, 13, Rost-9D, 7; Newscom: Javier Larrea/agefotostock, 29; Science Source: New York Public Library, 27; Shutterstock: Andrey Pavlov, middle (inset) 8, bonandbon, spread 8-9, Craevschii Family, top left 23, Jurik Peter, Cover, karamysh, background 21, Nattapat.J, 14, Oleksandra Naumenko, bottom left 23, Orange Deer studio, bottom right 21, Paopano, 17, Ravil Sayfullin, 25, Sansanorth, 19, Sergey Novikov, 5, Tatjana Baibakova, middle right 23, Titikul_B, 15, zizou7, 11


All internet sites appearing in back matter were available and accurate when this book was sent to press.

# TABLE OF CONTENTS

Words in **bold** are in the glossary.

# MICROSCOPIC MATTER EVERYWHERE

Everything you can see and feel is made up of **matter**. Your shoes are made of matter. So is a summer breeze. All living things are made of matter. That includes people!

The smallest pieces of matter are **atoms**. Atoms are amazingly tiny. They are much too small for the human eye to see. Take a look at the period at the end of this sentence. It is about 0.5 millimeters wide. You could fit 5 million atoms in that distance!

Talking about such small objects can be tricky. Scientists use tiny units to help. One of these units is the angstrom. There are 10 billion angstroms in 1 meter (3.3 feet). An atom is about one angstrom across. Parts inside the atom are measured in femtometers. There are 100,000 femtometers in an angstrom.

Atoms make up the ground, the air, and everything else around us.

Atoms have three basic parts. They are protons, neutrons, and electrons. Protons have a positive electric charge. Electrons have a negative charge. Neutrons have no charge.

Protons and neutrons are in the middle of an atom. They make up the **nucleus**.

Electrons move around the nucleus. Some diagrams show them circling the nucleus like planets around the sun. But this is a simplified view. Electrons actually form a cloud around the nucleus.

## SPLITTING THE ATOM

The nucleus of an atom is held together tightly. But firing a neutron at the nucleus can split it apart. This can release other neutrons. They fly away and split nearby atoms. This process is called nuclear fission. It releases a lot of energy. It is used in power plants and nuclear weapons.

Diagrams like this can be useful for thinking about atoms, but they do not represent how atoms truly appear.

Protons are tiny compared to an atom. If an atom were the size of a football field, the proton would be as big as an ant.

Protons and neutrons are super small. Scientists don't even know their sizes for sure. In 2019, scientists published a new estimate. They measured the proton at about 1.66 femtometers wide. The neutron is likely about the same size. Scientists believe that electrons don't have any size at all.

However, scientists do know the masses of these particles. A proton is amazingly light. It has a mass of about 0.00000000000000000000000000167 kilograms. Scientists write this as $1.67 \times 10^{-27}$ kg. A unit called the atomic mass unit (amu) makes things a little easier. Protons and neutrons each have a mass of about one amu. The mass of an electron is 1,836 times smaller than that.

Atoms are known by their mass number and their atomic number. The mass number is how many protons and neutrons an atom has. The atomic number is how many protons it has.

Atoms with different numbers of protons are different **elements**. For example, an atom with one proton is always a hydrogen atom. Its atomic number is one. An atom with eight protons is always an oxygen atom. Its atomic number is eight.

Atoms of the same element may have different mass numbers. The number of protons stays the same. But the number of neutrons can vary. Most hydrogen atoms have zero neutrons. Their mass number is one. Some atoms of hydrogen have one neutron. Their mass number is two. Some even have two neutrons. Their mass number is three. Each form of the atom is called an **isotope**.

# HYDROGEN ISOTOPES

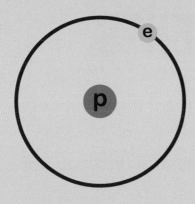

Protons: 1
Neutrons: 0
Electrons: 1

MASS NUMBER: 1
ATOMIC NUMBER: 1

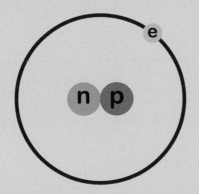

Protons: 1
Neutrons: 1
Electrons: 1

MASS NUMBER: 2
ATOMIC NUMBER: 1

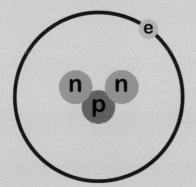

Protons: 1
Neutrons: 2
Electrons: 1

MASS NUMBER: 3
ATOMIC NUMBER: 1

# CHAPTER TWO

# ORGANIZING ELEMENTS

In the 1800s, scientists noticed that groups of elements have some things in common. Russian scientist Dmitri Mendeleev studied these patterns. He organized the elements into rows and columns. Mendeleev's chart is called the periodic table. We still use it today.

## CREATING ELEMENTS

Not all of the elements on the periodic table are found in nature. The elements with the highest atomic numbers are made in labs. Scientists smash atoms together to make them. For example, neon has an atomic number of 10. Uranium has an atomic number of 92. Scientists crashed them together to make nobelium. This new element has an atomic number of 102.

By 2021, there were 118 known elements on the periodic table.

| | 1 | 2 | 3 | 4 | 5 | 6 | 7 | 8 | 9 | 10 | 11 | 12 | 13 | 14 | 15 | 16 | 17 | 18 |
|---|---|---|---|---|---|---|---|---|---|---|---|---|---|---|---|---|---|---|
| 1 | H 1 | | | | | | | | | | | | | | | | | He 2 |
| 2 | Li 3 | Be 4 | | | | | | | | | | | B 5 | C 6 | N 7 | O 8 | F 9 | Ne 10 |
| 3 | Na 11 | Mg 12 | | | | | | | | | | | Al 13 | Si 14 | P 15 | S 16 | Cl 17 | Ar 18 |
| 4 | K 19 | Ca 20 | Sc 21 | Ti 22 | V 23 | Cr 24 | Mn 25 | Fe 26 | Co 27 | Ni 28 | Cu 29 | Zn 30 | Ga 31 | Ge 32 | As 33 | Se 34 | Br 35 | Kr 36 |
| 5 | Rb 37 | Sr 38 | Y 39 | Zr 40 | Nb 41 | Mo 42 | Tc 43 | Ru 44 | Rh 45 | Pd 46 | Ag 47 | Cd 48 | In 49 | Sn 50 | Sb 51 | Te 52 | I 53 | Xe 54 |
| 6 | Cs 55 | Ba 56 | La 57 | Hf 72 | Ta 73 | W 74 | Re 75 | Os 76 | Ir 77 | Pt 78 | Au 79 | Hg 80 | Tl 81 | Pb 82 | Bi 83 | Po 84 | At 85 | Rn 86 |
| 7 | Fr 87 | Ra 88 | Ac 89 | Rf 104 | Db 105 | Sg 106 | Bh 107 | Hs 108 | Mt 109 | Ds 110 | Rg 111 | Cn 112 | Nh 113 | Fl 114 | Mc 115 | Lv 116 | Ts 117 | Og 118 |

| Ce 58 | Pr 59 | Nd 60 | Pm 61 | Sm 62 | Eu 63 | Gd 64 | Tb 65 | Dy 66 | Ho 67 | Er 68 | Tm 69 | Yb 70 | Lu 71 |
|---|---|---|---|---|---|---|---|---|---|---|---|---|---|
| Th 90 | Pa 91 | U 92 | Np 93 | Pu 94 | Am 95 | Cm 96 | Bk 97 | Cf 98 | Es 99 | Fm 100 | Md 101 | No 102 | Lr 103 |

The periodic table lists all the known elements. The letters stand for the name of the element. For example, H is hydrogen. Zn is zinc. From top left to bottom right, the elements are listed by atomic number.

The rows in the periodic table are called periods. The columns are known as groups. Within each group, elements share features in common.

Group 18 is on the right edge of the table. It contains helium, neon, argon, and more. They are all colorless, odorless gases. They do not often react with other atoms. These elements are known as the noble gases.

Neon is one of the noble gases. It is often used in lighted signs.

Magnesium, a metal in Group 2, is used in wheels for race cars.

Group 2 is near the left edge of the table. It contains beryllium, magnesium, calcium, and more. These are metals with a gray or white color. They can conduct electricity well.

# BRINGING ATOMS TOGETHER

Atoms join to form **molecules**. Some molecules have just two atoms. Others are made up of thousands.

Some molecules contain atoms from a single element. For example, the oxygen we breathe is made up of molecules. Each oxygen molecule contains two oxygen atoms.

Other molecules have atoms from multiple elements. These molecules are known as compounds. One example is the gas methane. Each methane molecule has one carbon atom and four hydrogen atoms.

## FACT

In 2011, scientists created a huge molecule. They called this tree-shaped molecule PG5. It weighed the same as 200 million hydrogen atoms!

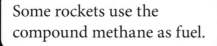

Some rockets use the compound methane as fuel.

To join together, atoms form **bonds**. The three major types of bonds are ionic, covalent, and metallic.

In ionic bonding, an electron moves from one atom to the other. One example of this can be seen in table salt. It is made up of sodium (Na) and chlorine (Cl). An electron from sodium moves to the chlorine.

In covalent bonding, atoms share electrons. Methane gas is an example of this. A molecule of this gas contains one carbon (C) and four hydrogen (H) atoms. Each hydrogen atom shares an electron with the carbon atom.

In metallic bonding, electrons move freely between nearby atoms. An example can be seen in sodium. This metal is made up of many sodium atoms joined together. The movement of electrons makes metals great at conducting electricity.

# TYPES OF BONDS

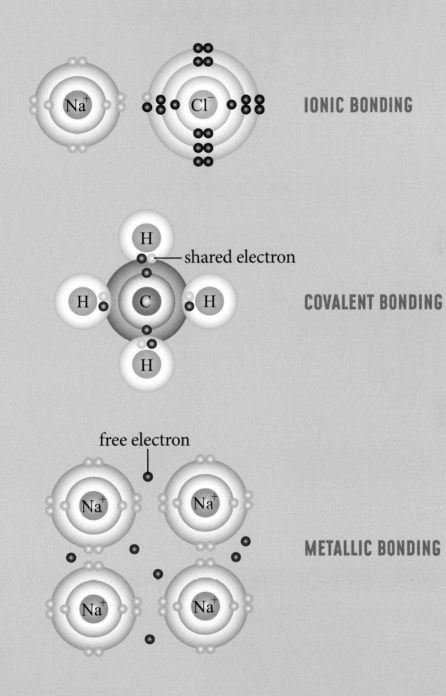

IONIC BONDING

COVALENT BONDING

METALLIC BONDING

19

# THE MOLECULES OF LIFE

Molecules make life possible. Living things are complicated. It takes a lot to keep them alive. A few key molecules are especially important.

One of these is water. A water molecule has one oxygen atom and two hydrogen atoms. The atoms form a covalent bond.

Water makes up more than half a person's weight. It does many things in the body. From the smallest bacteria to the largest whales, all living things need water to survive.

## FACT

A single snowflake contains around 1 quintillion water molecules. Written out, that's a one followed by 18 zeroes!

Water in liquid form fills lakes, rivers, and oceans. Water in solid form can be seen on snowy mountains.

The foods we eat contain molecules that are important for life. They are called nutrients. These nutrients include fats, carbohydrates, and proteins.

Fats are made up of carbon, hydrogen, and oxygen. Some fat molecules contain just a few atoms. Others contain dozens. Fats help store energy.

Carbohydrates are also made of carbon, hydrogen, and oxygen. However, the atoms are arranged differently than in fats. Carbohydrates are the body's main source of energy.

Proteins are made up of pieces called amino acids. Amino acids mostly contain nitrogen, carbon, hydrogen, and oxygen. Proteins build body structures. They also defend against infections and do many other things.

## FACT

The largest protein in the body is called titin. It is found in the muscles. It is made up of 27,000 amino acids!

Foods with fats

Foods with carbohydrates

Foods with proteins

23

Another key molecule for life is called **DNA**. DNA contains the instructions for how to make a living thing. Traits such as height and eye color come from DNA. Parents pass along DNA to their children. This is why kids often look like their parents.

The DNA molecule has a double helix shape. It looks like a long spiral staircase. The sides are made of phosphate and deoxyribose. Phosphate contains the elements phosphorus, oxygen, and hydrogen. Deoxyribose is a carbohydrate.

Connecting the sides are pairs of molecules called bases. There are four types of bases: adenine, guanine, cytosine, and thymine. Each base is made up of carbon, hydrogen, nitrogen, and oxygen. The bases always pair up the same way. Adenine pairs with thymine, and guanine pairs with cytosine.

All living things, including people, have DNA.

# STUDYING ATOMS AND MOLECULES

Atoms and molecules can seem impossibly small. They are far too tiny to see with the eye. Even a desk microscope does no good.

Still, scientists were able to discover atoms and their parts. J. J. Thompson discovered the electron in 1897. Ernest Rutherford discovered the proton in 1919. And James Chadwick discovered the neutron in 1932.

These scientists could not see the particles they found. But they could see the effects those particles had. The scientists developed many clever experiments to do this. Their work helped unlock the secrets of atoms and molecules.

Ernest Rutherford's lab was the site of many important discoveries.

Today, scientists can directly see atoms and molecules. They use a device called an electron microscope. It fires a beam of electrons at the object being viewed. The electrons scatter. The microscope detects the pattern of this scattering. It creates an image.

Modern microscopes can see amazingly tiny things. In 2020, scientists announced a new breakthrough. They could now see objects as small as 1.2 angstroms across.

The micro world of atoms and molecules includes some of the smallest things we can imagine. Studying these tiny objects helps us understand the world around us.

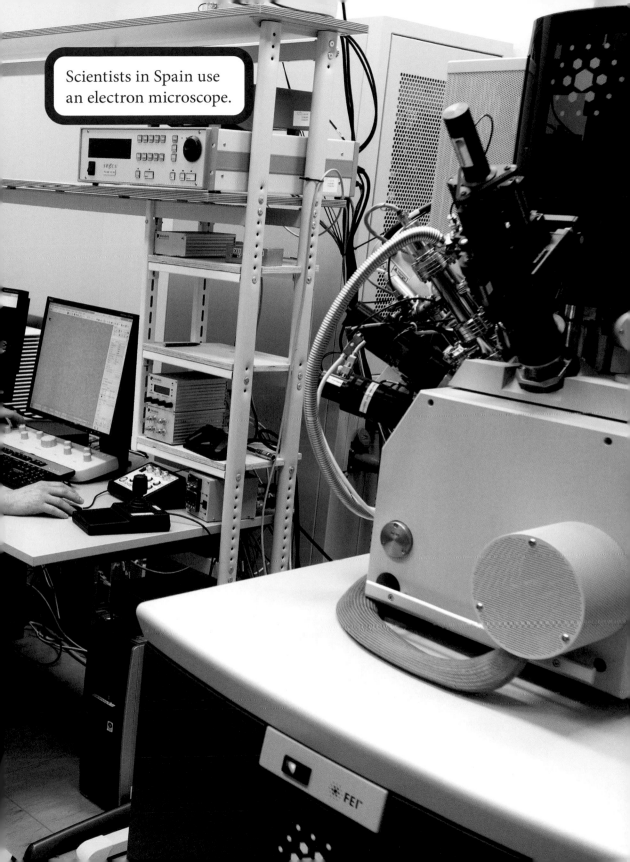

Scientists in Spain use an electron microscope.

# GLOSSARY

**atom** (AT-uhm)—the smallest individual building block of the universe

**bond** (BOND)—the connection between atoms that join together

**DNA** (dee-en-A)—short for deoxyribonucleic acid, the molecule inside a living thing that includes instructions for that living thing's traits

**element** (ELL-uh-ment)—a substance made of atoms that cannot be broken down into simpler substances

**isotope** (EYE-suh-tohp)—the forms of an atom that have varying numbers of neutrons

**matter** (MAT-ur)—everything in the universe that takes up space

**molecule** (MAHL-uh-kyool)—two or more atoms joined together into a single unit

**nucleus** (NOO-klee-us)—the center of an atom, which contains at least one proton and often one or more neutrons

# READ MORE

Biskup, Agnieszka. *The Solid Truth About States of Matter with Max Axiom, Super Scientist*. North Mankato, MN: Capstone, 2019.

Gray, Theodore. *The Kid's Book of the Elements: An Awesome Introduction to Every Known Atom in the Universe*. New York: Black Dog & Leventhal, 2020.

Jackson, Tom. *The Elements Book: A Visual Encyclopedia of the Periodic Table*. New York: DK Publishing, 2017.

# INTERNET SITES

*American Chemical Society: The Secret Science of Small*
acs.org/content/dam/acsorg/education/whatischemistry/adventuresinchemistry/secretscience/atoms/secret_science_atoms.pdf

*Britannica Kids: Molecule*
kids.britannica.com/kids/article/molecule/353479

*DK Find Out!: What Is Matter?*
dkfindout.com/us/science/solids-liquids-and-gases/what-is-matter/

# INDEX

## ABOUT THE AUTHOR

Precious McKenzie is the author of more than 30 books for children. Many of her books focus on animals and nature. She teaches English at a college in Montana. She is also a proud pet-parent to a flock of hens, three dogs, and three cats.